Living with Trust
Guidance for Your Life's Journey
By Alice McCall

Published by Healing Path Concepts
755 Grand Blvd, #B 105-162
Miramar Beach, FL 32550
ISBN: 978-0-692-75534-1

Cover Art by Pat Rinaldi
Pat lives in Flat Rock, NC with her lifelong partner Kevin Sweeney. Her
passion is to create spirit guided paintings and other forms of art.   The
energy of the cover art is "radiance, smiling confidence, deep peace, trusting
myself and my life's journey."

About the Author

Alice McCall is a gifted spiritual teacher and healing facilitator. In her practice, Healing Path, she works successfully with serious health issues and diseases. Her unique approach of working with the mental, emotional, and spiritual connection at the cellular level sets her apart from most other holistic practitioners.

In 2007, Alice was diagnosed with breast cancer. She courageously embarked on a journey of successfully self-healing without medical intervention. That experience led her to author Wellness Wisdom, offering an alternative view on health and healing.

Utilizing Skype, phone, and in-person sessions Alice helps clients globally to transform their way of being. With services ranging from facilitating healing of chronic health issues, to releasing emotional wounds, to practical relationship advice, to finding one's spiritual purpose - Alice has a unique set of tools to help clients in every aspect of their lives. She offers a free personal 30 minute consultation so you can learn about how she can help you.

Her credentials include: Bachelor of Science in Psychology, Masters in Business Administration, Certified Hypnotist, Ordained Minister, Certified Reiki I & II Practitioner, Certified Quantum Touch Practitioner.

www.HealingPath.info

Contents

Forward

Does fear keep you frozen in a life that you do not want?

Trust and surrender are what all souls have agreed to master and internalize as a way of being in this lifetime. We all have different experiences that challenge us – causing us to choose fear or trust. Most of us choose to live in fear by doing the same old thing that does not work or doing something to follow expectations. But there is another choice, one of seeking the wisdom of your heart and soul, to courageously step out with total trust in your life. Does this sound scary? When you first consider this choice it sure does feel very scary. However, when you chose to trust your heart's wisdom it always works out okay and usually even better than what you could have envisioned.

I used to be frozen in fear myself. I learned how to move out of fear and live my life my way, and so can you. This book is designed to help you trust your own heartfelt wisdom and to co-create the life you desire and deserve. It covers a lot of ground so you can feel good about taking the next step in your trust journey. It focuses on practical advice with many tips and suggestions. The best part is when you incorporate these tips and ideas into your life, you will feel free and unburdened. You will wish that you had embraced these principles earlier.

There is no need to read this material straight through. In fact, it is preferable to read it section by section with a pause of a day or two in-between for processing and integration.

I ask that you open yourself while reading, to let the information be absorbed by your heart. Your heart will help inform your brain of the truths that resonate with you as you travel the next portion of your trust journey – page by page.

Love to you,
Alice

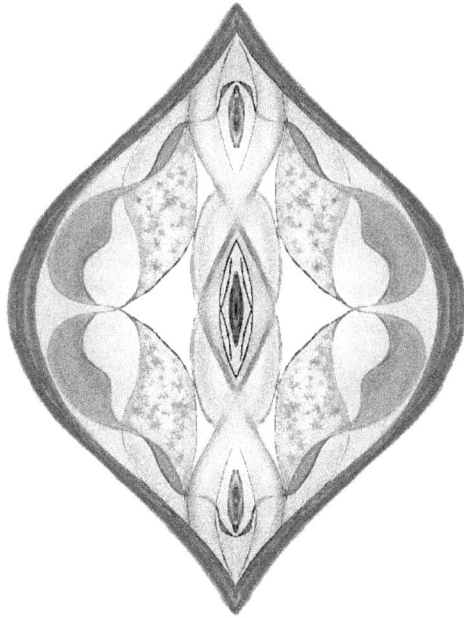

Introduction

Embrace your ability to live your life your way, by trusting your own true self.

Years ago, my spiritual guidance invited me to mediate and focus on centering myself within my heart. I was guided to do this so I could further learn about the inside me and the language of my soul. This opened up a whole new world for me as I learned to communicate with my true spiritual self, along with forming active relationships with my deceased relatives, Archangel Michael, the Ascended Master St Germaine, and more.

During the process, I was clearly told how all I needed to know could be accessed from the inside of me - the real me. I was directed to start bringing a notebook to my meditation sessions so I could take notes – to better retain the details that sometimes would become muddled as I emerged from my meditation.

The experience included instruction on how energy flows in the Universe and how to heal at the cellular and subatomic levels within the body, emotions, and mind. I also learned how to trust and use what I was sourcing from the deepest regions of my heart and soul to guide my decision making and beliefs.

Why is it important to go inward for guidance and decision making? The secret of moving towards a life of freedom, ease, love, and joy will be revealed as personal answers for each of us. It will not be found by seeking it through someone else or even by asking what we universally call God – as these remain outside of us. It is through connecting with your own self - a divine spark of God that resides within – that you will uncover your answer.

That means the way out of feeling stuck, despair, fear, or insecurity is not through another person or God outside of you, but through God inside of you. Your unique expression of God holds the key. The answer won't be found within your mind and emotions – but within the truest, most divine spark of your being.

The human structure/form includes the mind, emotion, and body. These are your temple - your house for this life experience, but it is not 'you'. At your truest form, you are a spiritual soul. This is the part of you that lives on after the body expires.

Understanding who you really are, allows you the ability to fully express the truth within you – your authentic self. You are able to stop searching outside sources for your truth and wisdom, as you can connect with it from within. It also means understanding the place of the human ego mind, and how it does not supply your truth and wisdom.

As I have traveled this path, I have come to fully understand how sourcing all wisdom from within is the most beneficial answer for the unique person that each of us are. This most easily occurs through your heart, as it is the spiritual connection to your physical body.

Sourcing your wisdom from within is so important, but its benefits are limited without your ability to trust it and yourself enough to use it.

Once a message from your heart is received, it is important to truly trust it. The combination of heart sourced wisdom and unconditional trust is how you can move from feelings like despair, fear, and being stuck.

Ask yourself these questions:

Do you trust yourself?

Do you trust others in your life?

Do you trust God?

Do you trust your life's journey?

Do you trust your ideas, intuition, and inspirations?

Do you trust that you are safe and protected?

Do you trust that all will turn out well, even when it seems that it will not?

Do you trust that you are always loved and cared for?

If you are honest with yourself, you will acknowledge that you answered 'no' to most or even all of these questions. The path before you is one of declaring 'yes'. Yes, you trust that you are loved and cared for. Yes, you trust your ideas, intuition, and inspirations. Yes, you trust your inner guidance.

It can often feel easy to trust in *anything* rather than our heart-felt truth. We'll trust what the TV says, doctors, a manager's judgment of us, a cab driver, the internet, or what our friends think before we put trust in ourselves. When a nagging awareness that a situation does not feel right demands our attention -   we do not trust it. Worse, we often won't even take into consideration what our intuition is trying to share. So we set forth on an opposite path only to learn, after the fact, how our inner guidance was right. Even after an experience like this, we still find it problematic to fully trust our own truth when it appears with a new message.

It's easier to trust in things you can see, so trusting those that are unseen takes practice.   It can even require mastering patience for occasions when things proceed slower than our human self would like.

Simply, human habits and thoughts offer the same limited results. Feelings of being stuck, unhappy, and unfulfilled start to appear as you forge ahead on the safest path that is guided by your habits and thoughts. The idea of trying an alternative source for guidance can produce extreme fear - so you stay with what feels comfortable, even if it means settling for less.

This book takes a deeper look at the many facets of what trusting the wisdom of your heart really means. It examines in practical terms how to live a different way – one with trust instead of fear!

I want to begin by sharing my journey of trusting the wisdom of my heart. I began trusting and acting upon the wisdom of my heart in 2000. Since that time, it has become my automatic way of living and being. I have learned so much by allowing myself to embrace a journey of trust.

There are many reasons why living with your hearts guidance in trust is an advantageous path – the benefits as well as the common missteps, obstacles, and challenges are conveyed in this book. I hope that it offers knowledge in your journey towards mastering a path of trust.

Follow Your Heart

The highest and best choice for being in each moment comes from the wisdom of your heart.

I began to fully follow the wisdom and guidance of my heart in 2000, when I made the decision to step out of my successful corporate career onto an unknown path. I was being guided to assist others to transform physical and emotional issues at the cellular level. This step into the unknown was *huge* for me. Although I had spiritual training in this area as well as associated degrees, it was a big change! I focused on being courageous and trusting, while I continued to listen to my heart for guidance.

Next, my heart led me to leave Atlanta, Georgia and move to an unfamiliar, sleepy beach town along the gulf coast of Florida. It was there my new life unfolded. My reputation grew quickly as my client appointments, speaking engagements, and publishing opportunities increased. Although I was still living day-to-day with my finances, life felt good and so did I. The unknown was becoming my new known.

Then, lightning struck in 2007. I received an unexpected diagnosis of breast cancer - ductal carcinoma, estrogen and progesterone receptive. I was fearful. Who wouldn't be? I was being pressured to follow the 'gold standard' traditional recommendation - to have my left breast and underarm lymph nodes removed, followed by a mix of possibly radiation, chemotherapy, and hormone treatments. They wanted me to do it *now!* My heart, however, wanted something else.

My heart wanted me to courageously step into the unknown again, despite my fears and the fears of those around me. My heart wanted me to walk my talk. My heart wanted me to be able to offer solid hope to others on how there is another way to transform health issues such as cancer.

We all have hurdles in our lives. When we are honest with ourselves, we may discover how doubting our self is usually at the top of the list, and it was certainly at the top of mine.

I doubted being able to be successful as both the healing facilitator and the client for my journey back to wellness. I looked directly at my own self-doubt and understood it as an opportunity for self-mastery. If my heart and soul felt I could do this, then I could. I had the proven skills, knowledge, and credentials - I just needed to trust the process.

I spent time to energetically shift the doubt that was present within me – clearing all levels of my being. Then I stated my heart's intention, "I intend that I will be guided to successfully heal myself of breast cancer, so that I can offer hope to others and share what I learn."

Five and a half weeks later - by using tools like my cellular level healing practice, guidance from God and the angels, hypnotherapy, and more - the inflamed, agitating energy that was diagnosed as cancer suddenly felt flat, neutral, and non-existent. I don't want to present this journey as an easy one. I was laser-focused on transforming my mind, emotions, spirit, and body through many amazing sessions with the inside of me. My total transformation was my singular point of concentration.

Although I had spiritual validation that the cancer was healed from the inside out, and felt the energy inside the lump go flat/neutral, the lump was still present. Just over two months later, I had medical proof of my transformation from a thermogram - a safer alternative to mammograms. The report showed no indication of cancer and I was jubilantly filled with gratitude.

Since my original diagnosis in late 2007, I regularly use themograms for diagnostic purposes and am happy to share that there has been no indication of cancer. My breast and lymph nodes which were to be removed, remain as healthy parts of me today.

I am blessed for many reasons.

I am blessed for the diagnosis of cancer that spurred me to resolve deep emotional and mental wounds within me. I am so light and bright as a result. Nothing gets to me anymore! This is a true gift, one which was made possible by my heart's wisdom and my choice to trust it. This journey uplifted me further on my spiritual path – and I'm grateful for the opportunity of self-mastery.

I am blessed because of the spiritual support I continue to receive.

I am blessed because my intention to heal so I could offer hope and knowledge to others continues to manifest.

My personal wellness journey has produced my book, *Wellness Wisdom*, several CDs, speaking engagements, articles, interviews, and many clients that I am able to assist with what I learned.

All of this occurred because I moved out of my own way, threw away fear and doubt, and followed my heart's wisdom with trust.

Am I suggesting that everyone take the path I did? Absolutely not! I am, however, a strong proponent that everyone should listen to the wisdom of their own heart when making important decisions. Wisdom that is perfectly tailored for each of us is sourced from within.

In recent years, my heart has guided me to the mountains of North Carolina and to South Florida – two locations where I initially knew no one. Although it seemed a little scary at first, I trusted my heart's guidance and settled into these communities. As a result, I am enjoying two communities that offer different experiences, personal learnings, and opportunities for me to share my spiritual healing practice. This happened because I listened to the guidance of my heart and confidently stepped out in trust.

Following your heart demands trust. The more you trust your heart's wisdom, the easier it becomes to act on it because every time the results will speak for themselves. When you follow your heart's wisdom things will turn out okay or even better than you anticipate. Each time you see those results, it becomes easier to release fear and move forward the next time guidance speaks.

Trust the wisdom of your heart instead of analyzing everything with your mind. Mental analysis can often bring 'analysis paralysis' because we find ourselves weighing all the options without acting. Although this can feel comfortable, it also creates a pattern of not moving forward. There is a graceful fluidity in trusting one's wisdom and being able to move ahead.

We each have a unique journey with unique experiences. Your journey with trust could include overcoming your fear of speaking your truth and trusting that all will go well when you do, perhaps it is saying 'no' to disrespectful relationships, or trusting that the next way to support yourself will show up. Whatever your journey is about, your worries and fears will only get in the way of your success.

Instead, try getting in touch with the wisdom of your heart in quiet meditation. Use what you receive to set your intentions for your journey forward. Then, stay in the energy of trust - trust that all will be well. When you give this a try, you will learn that all will go well. But more importantly, you will learn and experience a new way of living that is spiritually connected with who you really are.

What's Best to Trust --
Your Mind or Your Heart?

What do we do when we have a problem? The most accepted answer is to think through it - to trust our mind for guidance as we consider all available solutions. Yet, that isn't the only source of guidance available.

The mind has a limited perspective. It only understands the perspective of personal experiences and learned knowledge. The mind can only give you what you already know - facts, knowledge, and habits. Inspiration and wisdom originates elsewhere and are paramount to imaginative problem solving.

Wisdom and inspiration comes from one's heart and soul. They offer a broader view – a bird's eye view that is an unlimited beneficial form of guidance. This guidance encompasses what each person has learned, felt, and has yet to spiritually understand. It also includes room for inspiration from unexpected sources. It offers possibilities unavailable from one's mind, making it a much deeper well of wisdom.

The mind operates from Ego and is driven by fear. Often this includes the fear of making a mistake, of failure, of trying something new, or even of what others will think.

The heart operates from Love. Love is the essence of God and the essence of who you really are – the spiritual spark of God inside of your body.

Have you ever noticed that you repeat the same type of experience or relationship in your life? Or maybe you have the same feelings emerge repeatedly in your life? This happens because your mind is your creative force. When you only utilize your mind for decision making - it will keep giving you the same thing over and over.

It's time to try something new to have new results. Start by silencing your thinking mind and centering your attention to your heart. Then ask for inspiration – ask specifically about whatever situation or decision is causing distress. Wait and let the knowing fall over you. You will likely receive something very different – something that will resonate with you deeply and help you move forward.

If you decide to use the guidance received – be prepared for unexpected results. Use the information from your heart to inform your mind/thoughts and move forward with your creation. Take what you receive as inspiration from within - then use your thoughts, words, and actions to create.

Why is the heart such a great source of wisdom? Because it is more than a cellular mass of muscle that keeps blood flowing. It is an electrical transmitter and receiver of energies that is more powerful than the brain.

The heart is also the part of your body that is soul, spirit, and God connected.

If this seems odd to you, take one of your fingers and point to yourself. Where did you point? I've done this exercise at numerous workshops and speaking engagements and 99% of the time everyone points to their heart or chest area. Even your brain, which decided where you should point, knows that the embodiment of who you really are resides in your heart!

Each of us is a unique creation with special skills, knowledge, and purpose. Although it can be helpful to seek answers outside of ourselves - when we rely on others for their input or opinion we are receiving their perspective through their unique lens.

Information and wisdom tailored specifically for you can be sourced from your own heart and soul. I begin every healing session and guided meditation by connecting clients to the deepest part of their heart for that very reason. It is where I have consistently gone for guidance for myself for over 15 years. It is such a relief not to have to figure everything out with my human mind anymore!

How to Receive Info that
You Can Trust

The best place to access guidance that can be trusted is from your heart. The heart is a powerful sender and receiver of information – while also being connected with your spiritual self and with Creator God.

How do you go about connecting to this heart guidance in order to receive wisdom that is in spiritual alignment with your journey?

First, it requires building a relationship with your spiritual self and with Creator God. Healthy relationships are a two way street, and it is the same with your relationship with God and your spiritual self. A true relationship happens when we both talk and listen.

To foster a healthier relationship with God, it requires more than just talking. It's common to ask for help, favors, blessings, and 'pray to God' - but do you leave God an opening to communicate with you? God wants to guide us, help us, give us gifts, and share information with us - either directly or through others. However, we make it difficult when we never still ourselves to listen, when we never slow down enough to be present to receive. If we constantly occupy our energy space with doing things, how can God reach us?

Think about it: We are always surrounded with something to do, whether it is daily tasks, watching TV, listening to music, texting, talking on the phone, or being on the internet. Moreover, we are often guilty of doing several of these things at once! With this type of existence, are you really giving God a space to enter and be with you?

Life and the world we live can be very demanding, but creating a space for communication from God doesn't require a lifestyle overhaul. It is only a matter of finding a small amount of time each day where you silence yourself and invite God to communicate with you. If every day isn't possible, commit to twice per week or as often as you are able.

When you create a routine for yourself to be open, use intention setting, and center yourself in the moment – the communication will happen. It may require practice, but with patience and perseverance it will occur. Remain in the moment and trust that your intimate conversation with God will happen and that the answers you seek will come.

Take a few deep breaths, find a quite spot, and follow these steps.

Clear your mind and center yourself in your heart. God speaks to us though our heart, not through our minds.

Set an intention for your quiet time with God. Your intention sets your focus. Common examples are, "Thank you God for giving me guidance on….. This is important to me because…" tailor your intention to your journey.

Leave an opening for God to talk about something else that may be more important. When you use intention, include a phrase that acknowledges your openness like; "Thank you God for giving me guidance on ___ or some other area that you feel is important for me at this time."

Record the message/guidance received. Use a notebook or journal to record the message, knowing, or guidance that you receive. You may feel that you will remember all of the message, but it can be helpful to refer back to at a later date with clarity.

Trust the guidance you received. This wisdom is your truth, especially for you. It is more valuable and important than any thoughts, analysis, or opinions you or others may have.

Be in the present moment as you move through your day. God speaks to us through other people, experiences, what we read, see, and hear. Once you practice this, your intuition will kick in, alerting you when it is happening. You will be able to discern between normal conversations and experiences, and ones that are important messages.

It is most important, however, to tell God that you want a two-way relationship, and thank God for this relationship. If you do this and set up a routine that gives God a space to communicate with you, wonderful things will happen. Soon, it won't be difficult to carve out time for your conversations with God, because it will become more important than everything else!

When it comes to connecting with your Higher Spiritual Self – who you really are – it follows many of the same principles. Let your higher Spiritual Self know you want a two way relationship, and set aside time to establish the give and take. Utilize intentions for what you want guidance or wisdom on.

The best way to practice connecting with your higher self is by using the tool of meditation. Most use meditation as a one way experience – by quieting themselves through breath work and sitting in silence, then focusing on stilling busy thoughts. But meditation can also be used to access and connect with your heart, where you can discover wisdom tailored specifically for you.

Unsure of how to start? Follow these steps to engage in a meditation to connect with powerful heart wisdom from your spiritual self for guidance.

1.) **Center yourself with your breath**. Begin with closed eyes. Quiet the entire body, mind, and emotion parts of your self. Breathe deeply and slowly – focusing on the rhythm until a feeling of being centered is achieved.

2.) **Focus on your heart**. Using both intention and physical concentration, focus on the heart's location – the source of all wisdom and guidance. Bring yourself into your heart by using imagery and/or your focus, or better yet, just allow it to happen.

3.) **Use intention.** Intention setting sets the tone and direction of heart meditations. The intentions can be broad, vague, or geared to individual situations. An example of a broad intention is, "I intend that I will receive information or understanding that will be useful to me in my life right now." While a specific intention could be for guidance on any person, place, or thing that is weighing heavily on you.

4.) **Be patient.** It could take several attempts before beneficial wisdom and guidance appear. When I began my practice of connecting with my inner guidance through heart meditations, it took sitting in meditative state many times before I received anything. Consider the phrase 'develop a spiritual practice'. Like anything that requires practice, it isn't always easy or immediately gratifying, but with practice a rewarding, inspiring, and enlightening experience is around the corner.

5.) **Make a commitment**. Commit to the practice of connecting with your heart's wisdom. Listen to that inner voice and be disciplined about maintaining a relationship with that part of yourself. Changes in old routines will naturally occur as guidance from heart wisdom leads the way.

During heart meditations each of us may see, hear, or come to know the inner voice of our heart and soul differently. What is important is to get to know yours and to learn the language of your heart and soul. The language of your soul will be different from the language of another's – so it is something that you must uncover.

As your meditation experiences progress, the desire to interpret the experiences will magnify. Whether you receive guidance and wisdom through visuals, words, a keen sense of knowing, smell, a physical sensation, an emotion, or automatic writing – it is important to pay attention to what every meditation conveys.

Many passively observe their experience, but you have the opportunity to interact with it and learn what the experience means to you. Ask questions to further understand the message. Open ended questions like, "What does this represent?" "Why is there a white horse looking at me? "What is the message for me?" "Why do I suddenly feel angry?" "Why is my stomach suddenly upset?" "Why do I keep getting the word 'trust'?" These questions lead to personal answers and new insights.

After you ask the question, relax and receive whatever comes up. Be open to having a two-way dialogue with the inside of yourself. The process takes practice, but as you practice the information will come to you more detailed and easily. It takes time to learn the unique language of your soul and how to communicate effectively with it. And it is always important to use what resonates with you – your heart and soul.

Each meditation is different. Sometimes nothing is received, while in others a lot is received. The guidance could be simple and clear, or could need probing. When you establish a practice of being interactive with your meditations instead of passive - the information and decision making abilities multiply.

The best place to source guidance is by meditating with your heart, using intention as a vehicle for two-way conversations with your spiritual self or your Creator. It can be difficult to step out in trust, because of past experiences where you trusted advice from others or guidance from outside sources – only to have it not work out. As a result, fearful feelings arise when you are called to trust.

Yet this isn't relying on outside sources, it is trusting what you receive from your innermost self in sacred meditation with your heart. It represents a direction for you that comes from inner spiritual guidance.

Not all guidance is deserving of your unconditional trust. It is important to take into consideration how and where you are sourcing your guidance. The highest and best choice for each moment comes from the wisdom of your heart sourced in meditation. This is foundational to a fully formed trust journey.

Step Out with Trust

It is thrilling and rewarding to connect with one's spiritual self – something that can be achieved by utilizing heart meditations. As the heart meditation process unfolds, each person learns how to best interpret what they are experiencing and how to understand the unique language of their heart and soul. The gifts of the process include personal insights, guidance, and inspiration.

What good is this wonderful guidance if we do not use it in our life? This is where many of us fall short, because we are afraid to use it. We are afraid we made it all up. Afraid that trusting the guidance won't work out.

When you decide to use your heart's wisdom, there will probably be obstacles – both inside of you and outside side of you. These obstacles can make it difficult to act on the information from your inner guidance.

Why is it hard to follow the voice of your heart - your authentic perspective?

The whole world lives primarily from the mind - focusing on constant over analysis to assess the good from the bad. When we courageously step out to follow our inner guidance it can be against 'rational reasoning.' Further opposition from friends and family is common, because they are viewing your choices from a place of logical assessment. The decisions that your heart's wisdom may guide you towards are not always the most logical.

When I was diagnosed with breast cancer in 2007, I received guidance from my spiritual self while in a deep heart meditation to step outside of a traditional medical path and to use my own practice of cellular level healing to heal myself. Following this guidance, I successfully overcame my challenging diagnosis. During my self-healing many of my friends and family felt it was necessary to continually tell me how I was wrong, even going as far as planning an intervention. Although well intended, they were pumping fear into me on a regular basis, which is oppositional to being in trust and healing!

It is hard to move ahead with inspired plans when such strong opposition comes from loved ones. Just as it requires practice to listen to your inner voice, it also requires practice to trust that your received inner wisdom is the best choice for you at any given moment.

It is amazing how choices made with your innermost guidance always seem to work out, even when they are unconventional.

In 2003, I was facing a decision of moving out of a rental apartment and into a house I had built to sell – because the house was not selling. Logical financial analysis and pressure from family and friends all followed the same advice: I should get rid of the apartment, move into the house and once it sells find another place. It seemed like the logical choice as it would eliminate monthly rent – after all, I could end the lease but I couldn't end owning the house.

When I accessed my heart for wisdom from my spiritual self, I received how my heart did not want to move. It was too much packing, moving, unpacking, and moving again. My heart's wisdom also pointed out that I would be living alone at a construction site – this house was the only completed one in a new subdivision. This did not feel comfortable or cozy. I was worried and financially strained, but trusted my heart's guidance to stay in the apartment.

It was the first time I acted – or in this case didn't act – because of heart's guidance on such a major life decision. 10 days later, a strong offer came in on the house, and it was officially sold a short time later.

Because I followed my heart's guidance I was saved countless amounts of hassle, expenses, and stress. The opposition was real, but so are the results.

When stepping to the beat of your inner drummer, opposition will also present itself from your own habit way of being. This inner opposition originates from your ego and manifests as a fear, worry, or doubt. It is best to courageously acknowledge that those fears exist and then move forward in spite of them. With practice, it becomes easier to accomplish, especially as you experience the positive results from trusting and following your inner guidance. Not only will it always work out, but the results are usually better than what you could have envisioned!

In 2005, I was facing another financial problem with another house I was building. The contractor stopped working and wasn't communicating with me. I was paying him in thirds, and I had just paid him the second third which was to cover a good deal of work. It felt like he took my money and ran. I set intentions that he would make it right. I forgave him. I visualized him finishing the house, but it wasn't happening. Finally, I sourced the wisdom of my heart. I got four little words, "Let us help you."

I realized how I was defining the outcome, trying to create a solution that was not happening. I swallowed hard and admitted how I truly had not turned this situation over with trust. I got out of my way by saying, "I do not know how this can happen, but I intend that I will recover financially from this situation." Two days later a friend told me of an investor who was interested in buying the house uncompleted – so they could finish it to suit their personality and needs.

I never in a million years could have imagined that solution, but it was a perfect solution! Although I did not make money on this house, I received enough to cover all of the expenses. Instead of going into debt on a project that was looking grim, I was made whole financially. Moreover, I did not have the stress of finishing the project or trying to find another contractor to pick up the pieces. Yes, the results were better than what I could have envisioned.

I recommend creating and trusting the best solution possible for yourself and all concerned, instead of narrowly defining how you believe it should occur. When we keep our intentions broad, it gives the opportunity for God and the Universe to bring solutions that are invisible to us, because we are not blocking our energy field with narrowly defined criteria.

If trusting your heart felt guidance seems difficult, start with small, non-critical decisions. As you experience the ease and perfection of trusting your inner guidance and the gifts it yields, it becomes easier to apply to bigger decisions without fear. Each time the process will feel easier, which creates confidence and trust that the guidance you receive is true and in your best interest to act on.

Why is it still challenging to follow your inner voice, even when you have used this process? What could still be hindering your process?

The answer is essentially 'a fear of the unknown' - which is something that has been hard wired into most of us. Let's face it, when you make a decision based on inner wisdom, it feels like the unknown. It is a new way to operate and requires trust as the process unfolds because we have to be okay with not knowing what is next. Once you become comfortable allowing the process to unfold, becoming comfortable with the unknown, the process has room to rapidly manifest without fear intervening.

When fear is present, it is impossible to fully trust and surrender to the unknown. Whether it is the fear of not being good enough, looking foolish, not being successful, making the wrong choice, or countless others - all fears should be challenged so authentic trust can exist within you.

Many of my clients share a similar situation. They tell me, "I trust God and the Universe to do X, but it is not happening." That in itself is a worry – showing a lack of trust in the process. Worrying and being fearful works counter to your goals and hopes. When you are fearful that it won't happen – it is expressing a lack of trust.

As we challenge the fear in our lives, we each have personal triggers that will present themselves for us to acknowledge and overcome. Even those well on their spiritual journey, can find themselves facing personal fears. My best advice is to get out of your own way and not let fears, doubts, or worries interfere with the course set by your innermost spiritual guidance.

If you feel unhappy or unfulfilled and you are finding that it feels safer to stay with how it is, there is likely a fear or worry at play. A profound feeling of freedom and joy comes with trusting the wisdom from your inner guidance. Understanding that, will better help you become trust in action.

Living with trust is a journey and the process takes practice. All skills take time to grow and develop through practice – just as operating with trust does. Practice aids your ability to act on your guidance without worry or doubt interfering.

If worries or doubts begin to rise up, a simple process of breathing out your fears and worries, and then immediately moving forward with trust and courage before second guessing can set in - is very helpful.

Each time this process is practiced – your ability to trust and use guidance from your heart meditations strengthens – making the next time an easier experience. It will also lead you to the best choice possible for you in any given moment.

Surrender –
A Critical Part of Trust

We have all heard the advice 'Let Go & Let God', but few of us actually follow it. Many of us think that if we say the words, 'I let go and turn it over to you', that they have accomplished surrendering fully. However, there is more to fully surrendering as we must let go of all fears, worries, doubts, and concerns. Without surrendering your words are just words.

Why is surrender such an important part of trust? When we operate out of fear it's impossible to trust fully, because one cannot trust without surrendering, and one cannot surrender if they are fearful.

Surrender is more than a word – it is a complete action of yielding, turning over control, and allowing someone or something other than yourself to take over. The energy of worry, fear, or doubting the outcome interferes with your ability to fully surrender. Further, when you worry about the outcome you are demonstrating that you are lacking trust. Lack of trust is counter to your goal!

The first step to surrendering and trusting is to focus on eliminating your fears and worries, and stopping them from entering your being.

If you are like most people, you likely struggle with the need to be in control. It seems scary to turn control over to God. As you continue your inner work of releasing your fears and worries one at a time, the little fears will be replaced by bigger fears, and then deeper fears. Don't worry about it just keep shifting your fears, because if you do the work the day will come when all your practice and mastery pays off. The day will come when you can say, "Yes! This is what I have been building up to. I can finally do it - I am ready to relinquish control!"

This is great feeling and be assured that God is ready to help. This feeling is a very important part of the process.

However, you still have a role. Surrendering to God does not mean that you let go of your earthly obligations. It is important to do the responsible things in this earthly plane to help God, help you.

A practical example is if you decide to start a new business. God cannot get your business cards made or build a web site for you - you need to do these things. Once you complete the earthly frame work, set your intentions that your business is successful. Then, let it go and let God. Letting it go means you do not worry about how it will occur or when. Rather, you just hold onto the thought that it will occur.

If you try to help yourself by controlling everything, that could lead to a disaster. Over planning and rigidness does not allow an energetic space for God and the Universe to enter and assist. Why? Because you are clogging the space with your controlling energies - blocking all opportunities for something new to enter.

Simply put: Do your part responsibly without the need to control all aspects, and then release it. Let go and let God.

It is about balance. It you have a new business, God needs help to direct people to you. This will be difficult if you have done nothing to help your business be found. At the same time, if you sit all day, every day at your computer trying to make people respond to you - you are energetically blocking a breath of God's fresh air flowing into you. You shouldn't try to force things to happen - allowing is a better energy to hold onto and embody.

It is a co-creation process. God and you together. If you totally leave God out and take over, it won't work for the long term. If you do nothing and ask God to take over, it will probably not work out either. All relationships work best with balance. So, be responsible on this earthly plane to help God manifest for you, and then release it without fear.

It can take practice to find the balance point for you between surrendering and earthly responsibilities, but when you find the right balance that works for you – it does work!

Total surrender and trust of your journey is key. Surrender means turning over control, but it does not mean releasing your responsibilities on the earthly plane. A co-creation process between you and your creator is the answer. Listen for guidance and act on it, but don't start worrying and trying to make things happen. You do not know what the Universe is manifesting for you – it may look nothing like what you would envision.

As you include surrender into your daily life and practice it regularly – it becomes easier to let go of your attachments to fears, beliefs, and expectations. This healthy ongoing way of being naturally allows what you want for yourself to manifest faster and easier than ever before!

When you get the hang of living this way it is such a profound relief. You will feel a load lifted from your shoulders and a weight removed from your mind every time you truly surrender with trust or trust with surrender.

Discernment –
Is it Missing from Your
Trust Process?

The practical use of discernment is when we decide who and what information to trust. It is imperative to make choices based on what resonates within your heart and soul. It is also imperative to discern people who enhance your energy from those who deplete or agitate it.

Heart meditations are greatly beneficial for full discernment, but there is another powerful tool for discernment. Take time to honor how your energy feels while spending time at a certain place or with people. Trust this type of heart-felt discernment, as it usually is trying to communicate something very important.

Your heart-felt discernment colors how your energy feels. It is not about emotional feelings but something deeper. For example, if every time you are around a certain person, you feel exhausted or drained — your heart-felt discernment is communicating with you. When you feel relaxed and at ease — that is also your heart-felt discernment. This is a barometer that you can trust to guide you forward.

Although discernment is about making choices, sometimes the best course of action is going with the flow. When you trust and surrender — it is easier to be guided in the moment. There is a balance to be attained between going with the flow of life and discerning the best course of action for your journey.

When you only go with the flow, you are not co-creating or carefully considering who and what you want to be a part of your life. Personal boundaries fueled by your choices are very important to a balanced and successful life. Sending love and compassion freely to others is admirable - but equally, if not more important, is to choose who you interact with based on how they make you feel.

Trying to control your life will inhibit your ability to be fully present and receive God's gifts. Discernment helps you choose what is best for you, without trying to control what is not yours to change. It offers the perfect balance between going with the flow and applying choice to your life.

When we live in the flow without discernment, we can feel unfocused, unfulfilled, and lacking happiness. If you find yourself seeming to wander from one moment to another, unable to move forward, it's time to use discernment.

It may seem easier to live solely in life's flow because it is void of responsibility for what you create or choose to experience - but it leads to an unsatisfying life. Spiritually, we are called to be empowered and create our reality, not listlessly wander from moment to moment.

Part of this balanced approach includes letting God and the Universe know your desires and intentions when you seek to create a direction for your life. Further, it is best to source this direction while being in alignment with your own true spiritual self from within heart meditations. Once you discern in spiritual alignment and express your intentions, it is time to let go of any need to control the outcome - it is time to surrender to the flow of life.

Discernment is also powerful at helping you be true to your intentions, your desires, and what you're attracting/manifesting. If something or someone shows up in the flow of your life related to your journey, take the time to discern. Discern with your heart felt wisdom if this is really the right fit for you. Even if something or someone appears beneficial, ask your inner-self questions to be sure. Do their goals match yours? Is this the right move forward for you?

If you discern that the situation presented is close to your intentions, but just off the mark – thank God and the Universe for bringing this opportunity to you and then rework your intentions for additional clarity. As you restart the process with new intentions, surrender and trust again as your new intentions create, and discern with what transpires next.

Don't be stuck trying to make something 'close' work. Hoping that a situation or person will get better because it is the best option you have experienced so far - isn't the answer. Don't settle for less. You are worthy of having the best.

Life brings us red flags all day long, and it is our job to observe and use them to discern. They are powerful tools to help us move forward towards the best choice possible.

Remember your journey, why you are here in this human existence, is to know your true authentic spiritual self instead of your human ego emotional self. Once you acknowledge who you are, it is easier to honor your unique self by not settling for less or attempting to make a draining situation work. Have the courage to act on your heart's knowing. Discern and choose situations and relationships that support you - the expanded you.

The formula to replace worry and fear is to source spiritually aligned wisdom and then use it for your intentions, actions, and decisions. Next comes trust and surrendering – discerning the best choices as they appear in your path. It isn't about mentally trying to figure everything out – but relaxing and embracing the flow of your life. It is a delicate balance that helps you both move forward with your goals and breathe freely, enjoying the gifts of being in the moment.

Move into Trusting Your Guidance in the Moment

As I progressed in my trust journey – I had a shift. I was able to step out in confidence, using my heart felt intuition in the moment instead of needing to turn to a heart meditation for guidance. This does not mean I stopped using heart meditations, instead it marked a transition of truly trusting what my heart was communicating in every moment.

What does it mean to listen to your heart in the moment? Have you ever felt the need to stop what you are doing, even if you are in the middle of completing something important? Have you had the urge to do something outside of your normal routine? Or maybe you felt compelled to take a brisk walk or be with nature at a time of day that is unusual for you?

These are messages for you. Please take note of them instead of brushing off such feelings or doubling your efforts to focus on what you are 'supposed' to be doing.

These urges and feelings may be attempts from your spiritual self to catch your attention. Following where they lead can deliver gifts that can make an impact on your life – and possibly the lives of others. You could be guided to someone who needs your help, essentially bringing you to them; or maybe following the message will guide you towards something to spark your inner inspiration.

When you allow yourself to be guided, it welcomes new experiences because you are open to creating the space and time for them to become a part of you. Being open to this guidance allows wonderful things to happen.

Don't fight these waves, urges, and intuitions - adjust and go with them. They can help your business, health, relationships, and life! They could be leading you to a personal insight gained from quiet contemplation, the missing piece to solving a problem, or a person who can greatly impact your life – the possibilities are endless!

Whether your guiding messages come from your heart meditations or your 'in the moment' intuition - trusting and acting on your guiding messages is such a helpful way to live.

The universe works to put people and inspiration together perfectly in each moment. Will you answer the call of your guidance to connect with what is waiting for you – waiting just outside your planned routine or habit way of operating?

Allow yourself to follow the moment. Do not block it by staying stuck in old patterns and routines. All things are possible. Go with your deep heart felt sense. It is always right.

Being Trust –
This is Different than Trusting

It is a challenge to truly trust in God and the Universe. When we really, truly trust for the first time and it all turns out okay, we feel wonderful. We realize how life could have been so much easier if we had only trusted sooner. It is at this moment, we feel we have arrived.

Yes, it is a wonderful achievement and a great relief, however, it is important to keep in mind that surrender and trust are a way of being – not a single destination.

Trusting in God is not the same as *being* trust. Being trust is demonstrating how we are God's trust every day, by how we live, speak, act, and think. Nothing gets to us. It is the knowing that no matter what happens, it will all turn out okay; maybe not as we wanted, but okay or maybe even better.

Being trust each and every day is a high spiritual achievement and a wonderful, stress-free way of living. Why not move into becoming and being trust? The old way of worry, fear, and needing to control has not worked. Even worse, the old way can lead to illness and emotional imbalances. What is preventing you from a life of trust?

Know that this way of being is a journey. Each day something very little or very large could present itself as an opportunity for you to demonstrate your ability to be in trust. It is important to accept trust as a new way of being, and practice it at every turn. With time, being trust becomes a more natural way of living – your automatic way of operating.

When something unexpected happens or it *appears* to be negative, instead of worrying or being frustrated, ask, "Why did this happen? Why is this showing up for me this way? What does it represent? Is there a gift inside for me?" Inner exploration encourages fresh perspectives and answers, allowing you to stay in trust.

When we are truly in trust, we never doubt. Instead, we are patient. We live each day in the present. We know we are always guided, safe, and cared for. We know that our intentions are manifesting what we want or something even better. There is never a time when we should revert to our old behaviors and thoughts as that would take us out of being and practicing trust.

So what does all of this mean? Proactively it means taking responsibility for yourself, your thoughts, and your actions. Use your personal power to trust the intentions you have created - even if the timeframes are not what you hoped. Reactively it means not stepping out of trust when life brings situations and experiences into your path that are unexpected. Use your inner reflection to help understand their possible purpose and continue to move forward with trust.

Being trust means not doing everything, figuring everything out, or worrying. It means being able to walk through life with peace, balance, confidence, assurance, and love - that is something that all of us are looking for.

Conclusion - Spiritual Support for Your Daily Trust Journey

Here are my 'Four Steps for Spiritual Support' for your daily trust journey. Follow these steps, and then watch how things seem to almost magically fall into place!

1. **Observe:** Observe the signs the Universe gives you.
2. **Listen:** Listen to the wisdom of your heart and soul.
3. **Intend:** Set clear intentions so God and the Universe can support you.
4. **Step out:** Surrender and step out with trust and without hesitation.

First, observe the signs. Pay attention to what is happening around you. The Universe always gives us signs, but we must pay attention and recognize them. Let them be guideposts for you.

For example, if many of your relationships are coming to a close, that may be a sign from the higher order of things that it is time for you to form new relationships, perhaps ones which better serve 'the you' that you have become. If something you had hoped for is just not happening, no matter what you do or how hard you try, it could be a sign that this path is not for you.

Experiences that appear negative, can often represent opportunities to grow and expand the most. Once we reach the other side, it is easier to understand how those experiences help us to become stronger, and guide us to embody what is most important for our lives.

When we become an observer of all that goes on around us, we are more open to messages that are available to us.

Second, listen to your inner wisdom. Once you recognize a sign that is trying to communicate with you – it is time to check in with your heart and soul to understand the message. My preference is to do this while in the stillness of meditation, when I know I am fully aligned with my spiritual guidance. Ask questions to understand the message in its entirety, and how to best use it as a tool moving forward.

Make sure your wisdom and guidance is coming from your heart and higher self – not your ego mind trying to lead the way. Listen fully to your innermost wisdom, and follow the direction that it is communicating with you.

Third, set clear intentions. Now that you understand the signs, have asked and listened to your heart and soul, it is time to make some crystal clear intentions to help bring about your desired results. Make your intentions in the present tense, as though the result exists right now. Deeply feel the feelings associated with how good it feels once they have manifested. Then, surrender this creation to your Higher Self, God, and the Universe.

Fourth, step out with trust. It can be difficult to trust when you are called to step into the new or the unknown. Even though you may not consciously have a full understanding of what your life is evolving into, it is paramount to trust in the process, which in itself can bring you great comfort and relief. Yet, trusting without initiating can stall everything. It is very important to play your part and step towards your goals with trust. If you stay frozen in place, your efforts in the first three steps can be lost. It also communicates a lack of trust

Without trust, you are making a detrimental impact to your growth and to a successful outcome of your manifestation work. What we hold onto is what we create – that includes negatives like fear-based thoughts and feelings.

Stepping out with trust is always the best way to deal with the unknown.

Observe, Listen, Intend, and Step Out with Trust – these are the steps to support your trust journey. When you follow these steps, you embrace a life of pure, supportive light – and untold positive experiences. The Light of the Universe will be there to guide you, and help you embark on a journey better than you could ever anticipate.

My wish is that this little book has helped to propel you forward on a journey of using trust, living with trust, and being trust.

-Alice

A Message from the Author

In the introduction of this book, I shared how I was inspired years ago to center myself within my heart to source wisdom and guidance. It was here that I learned to follow my heart with trust. It was also here that I learned how energy flows in the Universe, and how our health and life experiences are often the result of what we have created through our very own thoughts, beliefs, and emotions.

All of this became the foundation of my ability to transform my health and of my ability to facilitate transformations for others. This work takes place at the cellular and subatomic levels within one's body, emotions, and mind. What is even more amazing is this approach leads to spiritual growth on all levels, along with the ability to understand and become one's purpose in this lifetime.

If my message resonates with you, I would be more than happy to speak to you directly through a free consultation. Each consultation is personal, addressing what you are interested in learning more about and how my work can directly affect you. This includes how I can help to you address health concerns, transform unwanted patterns and beliefs, grow spiritually, achieve your spiritual purpose, or to discuss aspects of this book that are important to you.

Although my practice began with transforming serious health issues, it has grown to include addressing feelings of stuck and powerlessness, enhancing abundance, transforming habitual fears or worries, improving self-esteem concerns, and more. Each session is individualized to address your unique concerns and problem areas.

Over the years, I have also developed a strong reputation as a Spiritual Ascension specialist. This popular term, means fully shedding your limiting behaviors, thoughts, and emotions - while becoming your authentic spiritual self. This is a freeing way to be!

I would love to hear from you either about your trust journey experiences or to schedule a free consultation so you can learn more about how I can assist you in your unique journey.

Much love to you,
Alice

Alice@HealingPath.info - www.HealingPath.info
www.WellnessWisdomHealing.com - 850-585-5496

www.ingramcontent.com/pod-product-compliance
Lightning Source LLC
Chambersburg PA
CBHW071424040426
42445CB00012BA/1286